NOT BY M

By Lanatha

MW01503275

Not By Myself. Published by Lanatha Johnson

First Printing: May 2020

Edited: August 2025

ISBN:9798643350903

All quoted scriptures are from the King James Version bible.

LanathaJ 2025

Lanatha Johnson clearly understands the stresses of dealing with uncomfortable situations. After experiencing different levels of trauma, she knows just how easy it is to think, feel and believe that God does not exist. But he does. Psalm 147:3 says, *"He healeth the broken in heart and bindeth up their wounds."* Lanatha seeks to encourage others to believe that they are fit for their unique purpose and that everyone has the potential to be and do their best with the moment they have been blessed with.

"And it shall come to pass, that like as I have watched over them, to pluck up, and to break down, and to throw down, and to destroy, and to afflict; so will I watch over them, to build, and to plant, saith the Lord." Jeremiah 31:28

Dedication

My granny Ms. Hattie Owens, my mother Ms. Mary Johnson and my auntie Ms. Lynette Owens, the loves of my life. Thank you for planting the seed of God's word in my heart.

Thank you, Heavenly Father, for blessing me with the courage to grow in your presence. Thank you for being my light and my compass. I now walk by faith because I believe you will:

"Lead me in thy truth, and teach me: for thou art the God of my salvation; on thee do I wait all the day." Psalm 25:5

Not By Myself

Preface

"God is good all the time and all the time God is good." Some way or another we find ourselves expressing these words when we feel the intensity of God's spirit. When we honor these words when traumatic situations creep into our lives, we must be faithful in our heart and believe that the Lord God is good all the time.

At times it can be very difficult to believe that our God will allow such pain and trauma to happen to his loving children. Yes, God will send the enemy after the weak and vulnerable but what the enemy does not realize is that the weak and vulnerable are already covered by the mighty hand of God.

"The LORD bless thee and keep thee: The LORD make his face shine upon thee, and be gracious unto thee: The LORD lift up his countenance upon thee, and give thee peace." Numbers 6:24-26

Offer your spirit unto the Lord so his good works can be manifested through you.

Contents

Not By Yourself: God is a peaceful and loving God. He created you to believe in the fruits of his spirit. Embrace yourself to be a tree that bears His fruit.

Honor Your Gift: Let God's will be done through you.

Throughout this book, the word "enemy" refers to Satan (the devil), not the persons who caused me to experience stress and heartache. It is only by God's grace and mercies that each person has been forgiven.

"Restore unto me the joy of thy salvation; and uphold me with thy free spirit."
Psalm 51:12

Introduction

Babies are born into families as an added abundance of love. Parents or guardians will make the necessary arrangements to provide a safe and nurturing environment for their new bundle of joy. But when there's evil lurking and tragedy strikes, unfortunately the little bundle of joy may become a victim of the enemy's attempt to leave a trail of lifelong shame and disappointment.

The traumatic situations I experienced as a child almost had control of my life. The emotional stress caused me to feel unloved and worthless because the enemy tried to make me believe that I caused those bad things to happen to me. Yes, I was living under the impression that I was the cause of my own pain and suffering. THE DEVIL IS SUCH A LIAR. God strengthened me with the power to shame the enemy.

"But rejoice, inasmuch as you are partakers of Christ's sufferings; that, when his glory shall be revealed, ye may be glad also with exceeding joy."
1 Peter 4:13

Chapter 1: I'll Believe It When I See It

"And ye are witnesses of these things." Luke 24:48

Children can easily be manipulated, and it is a shame to know that an adult will find ways to use a child's trust as an opportunity to prey on their innocence. In most cases, parents, guardians or caregivers may be unaware of the possibility of evil lurking in their loved one's environment.

I was mentally and emotionally stressed during the early stages of my childhood. No one knew how uncomfortable I was in my personal feelings. There were a few times when I had some things said to me and some things that happened to me that caused me to hate myself. I was emotionally manipulated into believing that I would get in trouble for allowing someone to "secretly" touch me. I was physically assaulted for not allowing someone to touch me and I was also deceived and cheated on when I "thought" I was experiencing real love.

During those times, I chose not to tell anyone about my feelings because I didn't think no one would understand or care enough to know what I was experiencing. I thought they would've also blamed me for allowing those things to happen. I was so internally broken at that time that I thought my life was normal.

Some parents or guardians may observe their child's behavior to get an understanding of their personality, but those observations can also alert parents that their loved one may be experiencing or may have experienced a dangerous activity. Parents who openly and positively communicate with their loved ones have a greater chance of encouraging them to also develop healthy habits of expressing their personal feelings.

As a young child, I did not understand what emotions were, but I knew I was scared and ashamed of myself. And though my mother instructed each one of her children to let her know if someone said or did something to us that made us feel uncomfortable, I was too afraid of getting in trouble, so I just kept quiet and the fact that I didn't tell anyone, that silence was the beginning of my internal brokenness.

When a child has unknowingly fallen prey to any traumatic situation, the damaging effects may possibly cause a slight delay in that child's emotional and/or psychological development and unfortunately that child will experience guilt and embarrassment which will also put them at a high risk for developing some type of mental or emotional disappointment or a level of depression.

In my early childhood and as a young adult, I was very unhappy. But God is an All-Powerful God because His glory destroyed the enemy's tactics to try and destroy my spirit.

"The LORD shall fight for you, and ye shall hold your peace."
Exodus 14:14

Another damaging risk of being internally broken is to try and pretend that everything is going well in your life. Not being true to yourself can or will be misleading. In other words, don't "fake it til you make it" because those fake moments can have a negative impact on your overall well-being that's caused by unnecessary or underlying stress.

Hiding behind my trauma and believing lies left me feeling numb and confused when I tried to "fake it" and I didn't do a good job of faking because some of my family members were under the impression that I was behaving as if I was "better than them." No, no, no and nope. Broken, broken, broken and broken is what I was. My family members didn't know anything about the stress that I was already dealing with and how their thoughts about my behavior made me experience a deeper sense of shame. I was so miserable that I would walk with my head down because I didn't want anyone to see my shame.

When I reached a point in my life where I was tired of feeling miserable, I attempted suicide. I felt like I had no reason to keep living. The embarrassment was too much for me to handle and there was nothing left for me to do. But God has shown himself to be merciful because the suicide attempt was just that, an attempt. The result I wanted to gain, which was to die, didn't happen because the spirit of God intervened. While I didn't understand anything about God and his protection when I was young, I'm so glad he knew everything about me.

"And in those days shall men seek death, and shall not find it; and shall desire to die and death shall flee from them." Revelation 9:6

For a long time, the enemy was trying to kill my spirit, but the grace of God rescued me from the enemy's death trap. God healed me and restored me. He needed me to glorify his name by sharing this testimony. God understood the reason why I couldn't tell anyone about those traumatic situations at that time, and he also forgave me for blaming myself for those unfortunate situations that took place. He also forgave those who intentionally hurt me. The word of God teaches that forgiving makes room for Him to bless us with the desires of our heart according to His will.

"The Spirit of God hath made me, and the breath of the Almighty hath given me life." Job 33:4

When uncomfortable situations happen, it may cause unbearable levels of mental, emotional, and yes, sometimes physical stress. The negative impact from any uncomfortable situation may also make it difficult to believe that God will use them to bring you closer to him in love and in spirit, but you must be willing to grow in faith through his word to believe it.

"God is a Spirit: and they that worship him must worship him in spirit and in truth." John 4:24

When you seek God's unfailing love and trust him to heal you, he will do it. That is his promise. I pray and believe God for you who is now reading this testimony. If you or someone you may know is experiencing or may have experienced the negative impact of any traumatic or an uncomfortable situation, seek God's will for strength and encouragement. Trust and receive him as your savior so you can embrace the power he has placed on your spirit because his healing power never ends.

"The eternal God is thy refuge, And underneath are the everlasting arms; And he shall thrust out the enemy from before thee; And shall say, Destroy them." Deuteronomy 33:27

At that early stage of my life, I didn't understand anything about the enemy's attempt to try to destroy my childhood and unfortunately my parents were not aware of those things that happened to me and because I didn't know how to express my thoughts or my feelings, I silently suffered from the effects of emotional and mental stress for most of my childhood and young adulthood. But I did not suffer alone. The Holy Spirit was right there amidst the stress and the fear that I was experiencing. He rescued my spirit and that is why I am now able to share with you just how blessed, grateful and thankful I am to honor Him for who he is. His grace and mercies endure forever.

Again, children can be the most powerless targets that can fall prey to the enemy's attacks. Since children are taught to believe and trust that adults will protect them while caring for them, that's what makes it difficult for them to be aware of or understand some of the evil tricks that adults will use to prey on their emotions and their innocence.

As a parent, you should actively listen to your loved ones. If or when they express any type of uncomfortable situation with you, believe them. Also encourage them to share with you what they know about God. Pray with them and for them. Observe their surroundings and try to create a safe and nurturing environment for you and your loved ones and continue to grow with them.

Although I've come to know God for who he is, I do believe that I will always be tried and tested because the enemy never sleeps. God's word says:

"Be sober, be vigilant, because your adversary the devil, as a roaring lion, walketh about, seeking whom he may devour." 1 Peter 5:8

The enemy's assignment is to do whatever he can to distract you from dwelling in the presence of God. Your mind and the mind of your loved ones is the enemy's playground. God need you to protect your thoughts and:

"Put on the whole armor of God, that ye may be able to stand against the wiles of the devil." Ephesians 6:11

Encouragement For Spiritual Growth

"If ye then be risen with Christ, seek those things which are above, where Christ sitteth on the right hand of God." Colossians 3:1

Since your mind is known to be the enemy's playground, you are encouraged to make safe and lifelong decisions by carefully thinking before you act or react. When you are not acting on the word of God, you are reacting through the enemy's tactics so make the choice to allow God's word to inspire you to align your thoughts with His will. Pray one for another because prayers never go unanswered. God knows, sees, and hears everything because the Holy Spirit is Omnipresent.

"²All the ways of a man are clean in his own eyes; But the LORD weigheth the spirits. ³Commit thy works unto the LORD, And thy thoughts shall be established." Proverbs 16:2-3

Storms, trials, circumstances, unimaginable and unforeseen situations will bring you into the presence of the Holy Spirit when you make the choice to seek him. I truly believe that it was in God's will for me to experience those situations because he knew they would prove how good and faithful he is. I am so grateful that God has blessed me to share those situations because they are no longer a stumbling block on my path. I forgave those who intentionally hurt me and by the grace of God I did not forget any of them. I know and believe that God has chosen to use my trauma to prove how powerful his words really are.

God Heals and He Restores

"But he was wounded for our transgressions, he was bruised for our iniquities: the chastisement of our peace was upon him; and with his stripes we are healed." Isaiah 53:5

If you are currently experiencing or may have experienced any type of traumatic situation in your life, the Holy Spirit is ready to supply you with the confidence you need to overcome your pain and to use your trauma to uplift his name.

"6For to be carnally minded is death; but to be spiritually minded is life and peace. 7Because the carnal mind is enmity against God: for it is not subject to the law of God, neither indeed can be." Romans 8:6-7

Do not let the enemy continue to try and put fear or doubt in your mind. Submit yourself to the will of God and let Him empower you with the strength that you need to live your life according to the purpose he specifically planned just for you. I honestly believe that the Lord has our best interests at heart.

"How precious also are thy thoughts unto me, O God! How great is the sum of them!" Psalm 139:17

Experiencing trauma is just one way of letting you know that the Holy Spirit of God exists, and a healed heart proves that his Spirit is real. Let the Holy Spirit of God heal your heart and allow his will to be done through you so you can let your light shine. God's keeps his promises to protect you from the enemy's attempt to keep you in darkness.

"And, behold, I come quickly; and my reward is with me, to give every man according as his work shall be." Revelation 22:12

When you encounter thoughts that's caused by emotional stress, you might try to suppress your pain by isolating yourself, but it doesn't matter where you are in your mind or in your spirit, God will find you.

"I went down to the bottoms of the mountains; The earth with her bars was about me for ever: Yet hast thou brought up my life from corruption, O LORD my God." Jonah 2:6

When you say that you are "blessed and highly favored", you are letting God know that you are trusting Him to be the highlight of your life. Your heart and soul are wrapped in His promise that:

"Thou wilt keep him in perfect peace, whose mind is stayed on thee: because he trusteth in thee." Isaiah 26:3

Chapter 2: Daddy's Little Girl

"Blessed is the man to whom the Lord will not impute sin."
Romans 4:8

A father's love can be one of the best feelings in the world. A father tells his little girl that she is beautiful. She eagerly waits for him to come home from work. She looks forward to telling him about her day at school, what she did with her friends and looking forward to him helping her with her homework. Unfortunately, that was not a part of my experience as a little girl. I remember my mother explaining to me and my siblings the reason why my dad was not coming home. Parents are supposed to be together forever. I needed him to come back home. I was his baby girl. I needed him to tell me that he loved me and that he was not going to let anything happen to me.

"Now therefore fear ye not: I will nourish you, and your little ones. And he comforted them, and spake kindly unto them." Genesis 50:21

My father's absence made me think that I wasn't pretty or smart and sadly that's what the enemy tried to make me believe. Can you imagine how those ungodly thoughts affected my emotional status as a child. Experiencing one of the most important stages of my childhood without my father left me with an empty heart, and I just didn't know what to do about it.

"I will not leave you comfortless I will come to you." John 14:18

Although my mother explained to me and my siblings why my dad wasn't coming home, it still left a negative impact on our life. My mother didn't have much contact with my dad, but my sister maintained her relationship with him. Unfortunately, that was not the case for me or my other two siblings. My sister was the oldest so of course my dad thought she was the smartest. My dad didn't love us, and I thought it was my fault that he didn't want to come home.

Again, those were my childhood thoughts, and I was totally unaware of the enemy's attempt to try and make me believe that I was the reason my dad didn't want to come home. As my siblings and I got older it became easy for us to understand why my parents didn't live together.

"For thou art my hope, Oh Lord GOD: Thou art my trust from my youth." Psalm 71:5

A father's presence plays an important role in the life of his children. Any painful experience caused by emotional neglect can or will develop into early stages of psychological stress which can also cause destructive behavior if it is not properly addressed. Depression can also set in and have a negative impact on a child's emotional development.

When the Lord took my dad's hand and led him home to glory, I did not cry, nor did I feel any pain or a sense of loss because of the emptiness in my heart. That same emptiness and numbness that I felt due to my dad's absence also made it difficult for me to believe that I would be worthy of experiencing real love or companionship from a man. If my dad didn't love me, why would anyone else? Yes, that's what the enemy tried to make me believe. And though the spirit of God was watching over me, I did not understand it at that time. Remember, this is my childhood story, and God has already forgiven me for not understanding his marvelous work and that's why I am so grateful to know and believe that God's love is unconditional.

"Then opened he their understanding, that they might understand the scriptures." Luke 24:45

When you've experienced uncomfortable levels of emotional stress as a child, it can also make you unaware of your weakness as an adult. And though you are to wait on God to fulfill the emptiness that you may be dealing with, some of us (women) will wait for God to lead us, some may choose to avoid relationships altogether and then there are those who will experience unhealthy or dead-end situations. But God's love is healthy and unfailing, and it lasts from eternity to eternity.

When I reached the age for dating, I **"thought"** I was mentally and emotionally ready to know what I wanted to experience in a relationship, but I was totally unaware of the enemy's tricks and schemes to try and take advantage of my weakness. Sadly, I didn't realize that I was expecting a man to validate me. I was expecting a man to fill the empty space in my heart by wanting him to tell me the things I needed to hear from my dad. Yes, the enemy tried to break me with that lie, and of course he failed. What a shame on the enemy.

"¹Hear my cry O God; attend unto my prayer. ²From the end of the earth will I cry unto thee, When my heart is overwhelmed: Lead me to the rock that is higher than I" Psalm 61:1-2

Women who never had a relationship or connection with their biological father may fall prey to the enemy's tactics. The real validation comes from the kind and loving words expressed by the Spirit of God. The truth in his words will always complement your life.

"The LORD hath appeared of old unto me, saying, Yea, I have loved thee with an everlasting love: therefore, with lovingkindness have I drawn thee." Jeremiah 31:3

God Forgives and He Restores

"¹⁰But the God of all grace, who hath called us unto his eternal glory by Christ Jesus, after that ye have suffered a while, make you perfect, stablish, strengthen, settle you. ¹¹To him be glory and dominion for ever and ever. Amen" 1 Peter 5:10-11

Our heavenly father loves us, understands us and he promised to be our greatest love. Since God created me in the image of his likeness, he is the complete source of my life, and his love will always be the greatest love that I need to experience. Although my dad's absence had a negative impact on my emotional development as a child, as an adult the word of God encouraged me to forgive my dad in my heart. God expressed to me that he did not hold my dad accountable for his absence and he also assured me that my dad understood the impact that his absence had on my childhood development.

"Make haste to help me, O Lord my salvation" Psalm 38:22

Communication, if possible, plays a very important role in a child's mental and emotional development. If there is little or no communication explaining the absence or separation of parents, a child will be left wondering went wrong and will possibly blame themselves (just as I did). Some parents may feel that it is not necessary to explain the absence, but I believe every child deserves an explanation. Again, my mother shared with my siblings and I the truth about our dad's absence which helped each one of us understand why they had to separate.

"To speak evil of no man, to be no brawlers, but gentle, showing all meekness unto all men." Titus 3:2

The word of God explains that forgiveness is the first step on a healing journey. Connecting to the source of my life gave me the power to forgive. God forgave me for blaming myself for my dad's choice for not making himself available when I needed him, and it was just that I also forgave my dad. If you make it a choice to not forgive, you are going against God's will for your life. I forgave my dad, but God didn't want me to forget. God needed to fill that empty space in my heart with his spirit, therefore I will always follow the truth that's found in his words.

"He healed the broken in heart, and bindeth up their wounds." Psalm 147:3

Since I missed the opportunity to forgive my dad face to face, I had to forgive him in my heart. God immediately started me on my healing journey, and I am enjoying the process. My dad has now gone home to glory, but I continue to pray with him and for him and this keeps me close to him in spirit. I know that he loves me, and I will always be "daddy's little girl."

God also needed me to forgive the enemy, the one who was sent to try and destroy me. But wait, I didn't do anything wrong. I was just a child and all I wanted was my dad to spend time with me so why did God need me to forgive the enemy? Well, I forgave the enemy because I had to be obedient. God also teaches us that forgiveness protects us while we are on or healing journey. If I would have made the choice to not forgive my dad or the enemy, God surely would have delayed my healing. I thank God for being a forgiver, a healer and a deliverer.

"14For if ye forgive men their trespasses, your heavenly father will also forgive you: 15But if ye forgive not men their trespasses, neither will your **Father** *forgive your trespasses." Matthew 6:14-15*

When you have a strong relationship with the Lord, you will experience greatness because his love is excellent. I am very grateful to honor God for the emptiness he allowed me to experience. Yes, I love him for that. He is greatly to be praised and will forever be in my heart.

"For this is the love of God, that we keep his commandments: and his commandments are not grievous." 1 John 5:3

Pray and ask God to restore you by filling the emptiness in your heart with his unconditional love. God need you to believe that you are worthy of experiencing happiness. Allow yourself to embrace God's joy by not continuing to fall prey to the enemy's traps.

If your biological father was/is not available to you, you can always reach out to your Heavenly father, the Holy Spirit. Be patient and take small steps to know your God. He promised to be everything you need so open your heart and mind and put your trust in him. What do you have to lose when you place your full trust in him? I am so glad that God delivered me from my old life and gave me a new one because his word says:

"Therefore, if any man be in Christ, he is a new creature, old things are passed away, behold, all things are become new." 2 Corinthians 5:17

If you trust that God will give you the power to live in him, let him lead you out of the dark places in your heart. Increase in your knowledge of his love and wisdom. When you accept the new life that God has blessed you with, the unfamiliar will begin to bring you closer to your purpose. Sacrifice, meditate on the word, and honor his will as he overwhelms you with his grace and mercy. His glorious and faithful presence is everlasting.

[10] For thou wilt not leave my soul in hell; Neither wilt thou suffer thine Holy One to see corruption. [11] Thou wilt shew me the path of life: In thy presence is fulness of joy; At thy right hand there are pleasures for evermore." Psalm 16:10-11

Embrace God's comforting words and allow him to speak to your heart and bless you beyond your imagination. Walk by faith and move with grace.

"And my spirit hath rejoiced in God my Saviour." Luke 1:47

Chapter 3: Touch Not Thy Dirty Deed

"Saying, Touch not mine anointed, and do my prophets no harm." Psalm 105:15

While some adults can be friendly and have fun with children, there are those few adults who are not so friendly at all. My mother always instructed my siblings and I to let her know if someone said or did something to us that made us feel uncomfortable. When the bad thing happened to me, the "evil man" told me that I would get in trouble if I told anyone, so unfortunately, I didn't tell anyone.

My mother's male friend always wanted to play a "secret game" with me. He would tell me the game was going to make me feel pretty and I had to play the game if I wanted to feel pretty. He would wait for my mother to leave the room so we could play the game. He would say things that made me laugh and then he would touch me. When he tried to kiss me and I said no, he told me that it was okay because it was part of the game. After he touched me, he told me to keep it "our little secret." Well, I didn't feel pretty. I was scared and I didn't want to play anymore. I wanted to tell my mother, but I didn't want to get in trouble.

"[17]The righteous cry, and the LORD heareth, And delivereth them out of all their troubles. [18]The LORD is nigh unto them that are of a broken heart; And saveth such as be of a contrite spirit" Psalm 34:17-18

The enemy uses friendly faces to target the vulnerable and unfortunately our loved ones will become the target. Sadly, I was totally unaware of the enemy taking advantage of me (that innocent little girl) and tried to make me believe that I would get in trouble for telling someone about the "secret game." And though I had been physically traumatized through emotional manipulation, the enemy has been shamed and defeated again. Yes, God is good all the time.

"For nothing is secret, that shall not be made manifest; neither anything hid, that shall not be known and come abroad." Luke 8:17

My mother told us that everything God created was beautiful and that included each one of her children. Now wait a minute and hold on, if God already said that I was pretty, why did he let that man tell me that the "secret game" would make me feel pretty? I did not like God because he let that man hurt me, but what a shame on the enemy for trying to confuse me at that time.

"But even the very hairs of your head are all numbered. Fear not therefore: ye are of more value than many sparrows." Luke 12:7

God knew that the enemy was on a prowl to try to destroy my spirit. I didn't understand it at that time, but the spirit of God was right there and saw everything. Even though God rescued me before the trauma got worse, my spirit was still in bondage because God needed to do more work through me. No, I didn't understand that myself, but God did.

"If thou afflict them in any wise, and they cry at all unto me, I will surely hear their cry." Exodus 22:23

I held on to that pain of being afraid and emotionally manipulated for years after God rescued me from those traumatic situations because during that time, I simply didn't know what else to do.

As a child of God, I was blessed with the strength and courage to forgive that man and to pray for him. I also asked God to forgive that man. If I would have made a choice as an adult to continue to hold on to all the hurt and shame that man caused me, I believe that the enemy would have tried to keep me trapped in a damaging and spiraling emotional bondage.

"Blessed are the peacemakers; for they shall be called the children of God." Matthew 5:9

Mental and emotional manipulation are just a few tactics that the enemy will use as an attempt to prey on innocent minds. When I told my mother years later about the "secret games," she was disappointed that I didn't tell her sooner.

Parents may be unaware of the manipulative tactics that other adults will use to prey on their loved ones. The man lied and told me that the "secret game" was going to make me feel pretty and that I would get in trouble if I told anyone. I was just a kid so what else was I supposed to do?

"But thanks be to God, which giveth us victory through our Lord Jesus Christ." 1 Corinthians 15:57

Everything God created is beautiful, and that includes each one of his children because he created us in the image of his likeness. When you surround yourself with the beauty of God's presence, you will not get in trouble for sharing your fear, shame or hurts with him.

"Fear thou not; for I am with thee: be not dismayed; for I am thy God, I will strengthen thee; yea, I will help thee; yea, I will uphold thee with the right hand of my righteousness." Isaiah 41:10

When I later learned that my Lord and Savior's trauma was worse than mine, and it was not done in secret, the very thought of my traumatic situations became painless. No, my unfortunate situations cannot measure to that of my savior's. That's why I am highly pleased to give God the glory for letting me win the "game" that the enemy thought he was doing in secret and for also blessing me with the courage to share this testimony.

Yes, I embarrassed the enemy who tried to destroy my spirit. But wait and hold on, while I still have your attention, I am more than excited to let you know that was not the end of my emotional stress.

It got worse and I am so glad to know God because I would not be able to share these next situations without his strength and encouragement. God and only God is amazing.

"When I looked for good, then evil came unto me: and when I waited for light, there came darkness." Job 30:26

The enemy was still on a prowl and unfortunately my family was the prey and sadly my mother was not aware of the enemy's attempt to destroy her family. While I was still dealing with the stress I endured from the manipulative mind game, my family and I almost lost our lives in a house fire. A situation that would have devastated my entire family. We know that fires kill, and fires destroy, but the enemy didn't know that God's eyes were watching over us and we were covered by His mighty hand. Yes, the enemy got embarrassed once again.

"I watch, and am as a sparrow, Alone upon the house top." Psalm 102:7

Although we know how children can easily become a powerless target for the enemy's manipulative mind games, adults can also become a vulnerable target without being aware of it. It was unfortunate that I didn't realize that my mother was a target, but of course I wouldn't have known that when I was a child.

"The eyes of the Lord are in every place, beholding the evil and the good." Proverbs 15:3

For a long time, it was just mom and her 4 children. My mother started dating a man that my siblings and I saw as being very scary. Not only was this man scary, but he was also evil with a horrible attitude. He would always fuss at my mother and accuse her of being with other men. One day when my mother left the house, this evil man started asking me and my siblings where she was going, we told him that we didn't know. Of course, he didn't believe us, and that's when he started yelling at us. What he did next was unimaginable. He intentionally set our house on fire, and I watched him do it. Unbelievable. He rolled some newspapers, lit them on the stove and put the burning paper on a bed.

I managed to run up to the second floor to let my other family members know that the house was on fire. When my aunt tried to see what was going on, he started yelling and fussing at her and then he hit her. It was by God's grace and mercies that everyone made it safely out of the house. Sadly, my aunt had to be taken to the hospital.

When my mother arrived back home, she tried to go inside to make sure everyone made it safely out of the house. The evil man was taken away in a police car and off to jail he went.

We had to live with others until my mother was able to find us another house to live in. We had a lot of nice neighbors who gave us some things to put in our new house. When we went back to school, some of the teachers also gave us some things to put in our new house.

Yes, our house burned down, we lost everything that was in it, but my family and I survived because the Spirit of God made sure we all made it out safely.

"The Lord shall preserve thee from all evil: He shall preserve thy soul." Psalm 121:7

When we went to the courthouse, I told the judge everything the evil man did but the evil man kept saying that he didn't do anything wrong and he wasn't the one who started the fire. I didn't understand why the evil man was lying but of course the judge didn't believe him so back to jail he went. He was gone, far away. We didn't have to worry about him anymore. Well, at least that's what we thought. We learned that my mother was visiting that evil man while he was in jail. Why did she need to talk to him? He tried to kill her family. Did she love us? If she did, she shouldn't talk to him.

Now wait and hold on, I thought since my mother always talked about God, why did God let her talk to that evil man? What God revealed to me (as an adult) was that children are not the only ones who are vulnerable. My mother was also susceptible to the enemy's attack. That's how the evil man was able to manipulate her and took advantage of her. Unbelievable.

"And lead us not into temptation, but deliver us from evil." Matthew 6:13

My mother strongly believed in God, but she was still vulnerable to the enemy's attacks. She never gave up on God and God never gave up on her.

"Be strong and of a good courage, fear not, nor be afraid of them: for the Lord thy God, he is it that doth go with thee; he will not fail thee, nor forsake thee." Deuteronomy 31:6

She finally stopped talking to the evil man. At that time, my mother may not have realized that she was a target, but she continued to pray to God. When my mother shared some things with me that she experienced in her childhood, I understood just how easy it is to become a victim of the enemy's attacks and why it was important to always pray and trust God in everything.

When I was just a child, I found it difficult to understand how God could love us and let bad things happen. If God loved us, he would not let bad things happen to us. Again, that was the lie the enemy tried to make be believe.

"He that loveth not, knoweth not God; for God is love." 1 John 4:8

We know that secret games and fires can cause lifelong emotional stress, but we also know that when the Holy Spirit of God intervenes, emotional stress caused by any type of traumatic situation will not have a chance to manifest in the heart of His children.

"And I was with you in weakness, and in fear, and in trembling." 1 Corinthians 2:3

Again, the spirit of God was there to protect me and my family from the danger of being killed in that house fire. I'll never know if my mother forgave that man for intentionally trying to kill her family, but I forgave him. I would have never thought in my years of living that I would have the heart to forgive anyone who chooses to intentionally cause harm, but God's word instructs us to be obedient and forgiving. These are just a few of God's many commands. Not only did I forgive that man, but I also prayed for him because God *"sendeth rain on the just and the unjust" Matthew 5:45*

"¹³For it is God which worketh in you both to will and to do of his good pleasure; ¹⁴Do all things without murmuring and disputing." Philippians 2:13-14

It may be difficult to believe that you can be healed from any type of traumatic situation, but you must believe that it is the power of the Holy Spirit that will heal you and use your situation to prove how good God is. If I didn't experience those situations, I will honestly admit that I don't know what my life would be like on this day. I continue to bless the name of the Lord because without Him, I would not have this testimony to share with you. We know that every traumatic situation is different, but the results of the enemy is the same and that is *"to kill, to steal and to destroy." John 10:10*

"It is God that girdeth me with strength; and maketh my way perfect." Psalm 18:32

Let the Holy Spirit of God set your soul on fire, and let the heat from the flames, which is God's word, protect you and keep you close to the savior. Your life has more value than you can ever imagine. Be patient and allow God to move you through your situation. Bless the name of the Lord and know that he will keep you safe.

"19To deliver their soul from death and keep them alive in famine; 20Our soul waiteth for the Lord: he is our help and our shield." Psalm 33:19-20

Although my unforeseen situations caused me to be afraid as a child, I believe that God protected me from experiencing the damaging effects of mental and emotional destruction which would have been a result of giving the enemy control my thoughts. This testimony is proof that the DEVIL IS SUCH A LIAR.

"Lest Satan should get an advantage of us: for we are not ignorant of his devices." 2 Corinthians 2:11

Our healing is a result of uplifting our thoughts, standing firm on God's word and acknowledging his presence. He needs each of us to trust Him in the process because he only wants the best for us.

Chapter 4: Mom and Her 4 Children

"Give her of the fruit of her hands; and let her own works praise her in the gates." Proverbs 31:31

One of the greatest things I've respected most about my mother was her love for God but what I didn't understand (as a child) was how did she love someone that she couldn't see? How did she know where he was? And how did he know where she was? Why would she love someone who let her struggle? Well, if I couldn't see the God my mother loved and who allowed her to struggle to care for her 4 children, I didn't want to know her God. Shame on the enemy again because I now understand that God is Omnipresent.

"23Am I a God at hand, saith the LORD, and not a God afar off? 24Can any hide himself in secret places that I shall not see him? Saith the LORD. Do not I fill heaven and earth? Saith the LORD." Jeremiah 23:23-24

I couldn't imagine some of the things my mother may have been experiencing as a single parent, but I do know that she did an exceptional job caring for her 4 children. And though she struggled a little bit, she did everything to the best of her ability to create a safe and nurturing home environment for each one of us. There was very little help from my dad, but she was still able to provide us with our needs.

"Not that I speak in respect of want: for I have learned, in whatsoever state I am, therewith to be content." Philippians 4:11

There were some scary times when we had to go to the doctor because my mother wanted to make sure we were all in good health. Well, I did not like doctors (and I still don't). I remember when my mother took me for my regular visit, and we thought everything was okay. When the doctor came to our house later that same evening, they told my mother they needed me to go back to the hospital with them and I had to stay there for the night, so off to the hospital I went.

When my mother arrived at the hospital, she didn't understand what was going on. She was upset because they put "extra" blood in my body without her permission. Yes, they gave me a blood transfusion. The doctor told her that they had to give me the "extra" blood because I had a very low blood count, (I had no idea what that meant) and if they were not able to get me back to the hospital to get the "extra" blood, it was a possibility that I could have died. What? I had blood in my body so how was my blood low? I didn't feel sick so how was I going to die? I was scared and I didn't know what was going on. I didn't want "extra" blood in my body, but I guess I didn't have no other choice. I stayed at the hospital for a few days until the doctors said it was okay for me to go home. I guess doctors weren't as bad or scary as I thought because I was able to get all the snacks I wanted.

My mother tried to explain to me how God saved my life. How? I didn't see God come in the hospital so how did he know I was there. I was too young to understand it at that time but as I got older, I learned just how God is always on time. He made it possible for me to get some "extra" blood. All praises to the Father of Glory.

Although my mother was upset that the doctors didn't wait for her to give them permission to give me a blood transfusion, she said she was thankful that God didn't "take" me away from her.

"He shall redeem their soul from deceit and violence: and precious shall their blood be in his sight." Psalm 72:14

My siblings and I had a great relationship for most of our upbringing. There were a few times when my brothers and I had several disagreements and fights. I always thought my brothers enjoyed bullying me, but I later learned that their behavior was only to protect me.

I never told my brothers about the kids in school who were teasing and bullying me because I didn't want them to get in trouble. It was difficult for me to concentrate on my schoolwork because the kids were always teasing me. Sometimes I would pretend to be sick just so I wouldn't have to go to school and hear the mean words from those kids. I never told my mother about those kids teasing me because I didn't think she would care. And though we had nurturing home environment, the outside environment had a negative impact on some of the stress I was experiencing. My mother would often move to different neighborhoods but relocating didn't make it any easier for me or my siblings. The same things continued to happen at the new schools, teasing, bullying and name calling but I still had to go to school and tolerate those kids.

Was I doing something wrong that made people hate me? My dad didn't love me, the secret games made me feel bad, the house fire, the issue with low blood, and the kids at school. Was I that bad of a person that I gave people a reason to dislike me? I had gotten so uncomfortable with my life that I really began to believe that I was worthless. I wanted to run away from home, but I was too afraid and didn't know where to go. When I got home from school, I just stayed in my room because I didn't want anyone to know how much I hated myself. But the enemy is a liar again. God loves everything he created and that included me.

Negative behavior such as bullying and teasing from other children and sometimes adults can cause your loved one to develop a high level of emotional stress, and this may also cause your loved one to purposefully harm themselves or someone else. Although I was a sad child who experienced those nightmares, the spirit of God was watching over me. Just a little reminder that this is my past and I did not know how to acknowledge God's presence in those stressful situations. God delivered me and encouraged me to share his great works. He will also encourage you when you bless his name.

"When Christ, who is our life, shall appear, then shall ye also appear with him in glory." Colossians 3:4

I remember when my mother started taking us to church so we could learn about the Holy Spirit of God and Jesus Christ, but we were too young and really couldn't understand that *stuff*. The church people would scream and make weird scary noises. I did not like going to church because I thought those people were crazy. My mother told us that was how people praised and worshipped God. The people were screaming at the air because I never saw God come in the church. Of course we had to attend Sunday school. Boring and no I didn't pay attention because I was not going to be crazy like those people. If I couldn't see God, how could he see me? That *stuff* was for weirdos. Well, I was a child when the enemy tried to make me believe that lie.

"Behold, he cometh with clouds; and every eye shall see him, and they also which pierced him: and all kindreds of the earth shall wail because of him. Even so, Amen" Revelation 1:7

I may not have paid too much attention to everything that was being taught in Sunday school, but I did remember hearing the teacher say that God is a spirit, and that truth turned out to be one of the greatest experiences in my life.

"Those who worship me must worship me in spirit and in truth." John 4:24

Although my mom struggled just a little, she faithfully prayed to God every day, and he lovingly provided her with everything she needed. I will forever be grateful that my mother continued to teach us how to pray even though we didn't understand any of it at that time.

When you make the choice to honor the spirit of God for who he is, he will keep his promise to comfort you in your time of need. I now move and live in his word, and I thank God for Jesus because he said:

"For in him we live, and move, and have our being; as certain also of your own poets have said, For we are also his offspring." Acts 17:28

God blessed my mother with a beautiful spirit and his excellent word proved that she belonged to him and not us. She has now gone home to glory, and I continue to pray for her and with her. This keeps me close to her in spirit. I thank God for being the source of her strength and the light on her spiritual path.

"2In my father's house are many mansions; if it were not so, I would have told you. I go to prepare a place for you. 3And if I go and prepare a place for you, I will come again, and receive you unto myself: that where I am, there ye may be also." John 14:2-3

God's word teaches us that we are just visitors here on earth. He wants to guide you out of your trauma and into his will for your life while you're here. He is ready for you to live on Purpose.

Chapter 5: Try, Try Again

"And that thou shouldest visit him every morning and try him every moment." Job 7:18

As I approached my early "tweens", I tried to feel a little better about myself. I just wanted to be a typical "tweenager," hanging out with friends, telling jokes and just having fun. Sadly, one of those friends wasn't so friendly. I lived in a different neighborhood, so I had to ride the public transportation to get back home. When it was time for me to head home, one of the "friends" wanted to walk me to the bus stop. While we were walking, he was still telling jokes, so I wasn't aware of his intention to hurt me.

"He was unto me as a bear lying in wait, and as a lion in secret places." Lamentations 3:10

While we were walking, some of the things he was making jokes about made me feel uncomfortable. When I told him that his jokes weren't funny, he grabbed me, pushed me down and took advantage of me. Unfortunately, there was no one around that heard me screaming. After he took advantage of me, he got up and ran. I didn't know what else to do so I just laid there feeling scared and dirty. I finally got up and made my way home. After this "friend" forced himself on me, not only did I feel more ashamed of myself, but the agonizing embarrassment was torturing. After that situation happened, I found myself not wanting to be around anybody because I didn't want them to see how miserable and worthless I was.

What kind of life was I supposed to be living? I had no friends and the ones I thought were my friends just wanted to hurt me. When I made attempts to be around people, I would feel nothing but shame and embarrassment so I decided at that time to just isolate myself from others so I wouldn't get hurt again.

"Who comforteth us in all our tribulation, that we may be able to comfort them which are in any trouble, by the comfort wherewith we ourselves are comforted of God." 2 Corinthians 1:4

Isolation, after a while, made me feel lonely so I forced myself to be around people because I didn't think that anything else would go wrong. so I made another attempt to make new friends. While hanging out with my new friends, my female friend wanted me to meet one of her male friends that lived in her neighborhood. These friends and I were having lots of fun, and her male friend began to express his interest in me and wanted just the two of us to spend time together. I really thought the guy was interested in me because he always said nice things to me. It was then that I learned that the things he was saying was only to get me to share my "self" with him. When I kept saying no, that's when the nightmares begin again. Why did these guys want to hurt me? What was I doing wrong? He kept trying to take down my shorts and while I was fighting him off, he started squeezing my hand and threatening to break my fingers if I kept trying to stop him. Then another unimaginable thing happened. He reached for a yardstick and started hitting me with it. He didn't stop until he got what he wanted. After he finished his "business", I left his house with huge bruises on my arms and legs from being struck with that yardstick. I felt like my life was over. I was already feeling ashamed of myself and at that point I really began to believe that I was worthless. Though I wasn't physically dead, I felt numb and lifeless. How could this happen to me again? Was I treating these guys bad? It must have been obvious that I hated myself and they felt the need to cause me more pain. I was so traumatized that I simply didn't want to live anymore.

"Therefore now, O Lord, take, I beseech thee, my life from me; for it is better for me to die than to live." Jonah 4:3

I tried to hide behind everything that happened to me. I tried to block the pain that I was experiencing by pretending as if that those things never happened, but the pain and embarrassment was there, and it wouldn't go away.

"Consider and hear me, O Lord my God, lighten mine eyes lest I sleep the sleep of death." Psalm 13:3

A couple of years after that nightmare happened, I saw this young man again. My cousin and I were leaving a neighborhood carnival, and he offered to give us a ride home. I wasn't expecting this guy to act crazy again but while he was driving, he was trying to make me touch his "self". Scared once again. Unfortunately, I couldn't get my cousin's attention because she was sitting in the back seat and didn't know what was going on. When he finally let go of my fingers, I was able to jump out of the car. Yes, while it was moving. I ran to a house screaming for help, but no one came out to help me. I continued to run, but he caught me and made me get back in the car. I was crying and scared when he finally took us home, that's when I told my cousin what happened.

After that scary situation happened, I had no desire to keep living. I was tired of being mistreated and taken advantage of. I cried for a long time trying to understand why I was being abused. I wasn't treating anyone badly so why did people feel the need to mistreat me? I felt lifeless and miserable. I hated myself and I really wanted my life to end. But oh, how I appreciate the loving Spirit of God because he showed up right on time to protect me from one of the enemy's most dangerous traps, suicide. Of course, at that time I didn't realize it.

I grabbed a bottle of pills and tried to take them. Yes, it was over for me. I put the pills in my mouth, but they got stuck in my throat. I spit them out and tried to swallow them again, but they got stuck. Why was it so hard for me to swallow those pills? I didn't want to live anymore. I was tired of hurting. I tried to take them again, and yes, they got stuck, so I just spit them out and threw them away. I stayed in my room and cried for the rest of the night. What else could go wrong? I hated myself and everybody else hated me too, even the God my mother tried to tell me about. At that point, I knew I was worthless, and I didn't care about anything else that happened to me. Yes, the enemy of God's creation tried to make me believe that lie.

"The trouble of my heart are enlarged: O bring me out of my distresses." Psalm 25:17

In my late teens, I started hanging out and drinking. I made sure I was never alone with any guys because I was afraid of being taken advantage of. Even though I hated myself, I was still careful enough to not let anyone hurt me. And yes, I was pretending to be OK.

After a few years of being uncomfortable from trying to do what everyone else was doing, I started doing different things. I started focusing more on school because I didn't want to be a high school drop-out. I took extra classes during summer break to earn the credits I needed to finish high school. I started my first job. McDonald's.

My mother met this great guy who encouraged me to work and finish school. Although I was happy with the new things I was doing, I was still feeling miserable and depressed. Guys would always tell me how beautiful and nice I was and of course, I didn't believe them. If I was so beautiful and nice, why did those other guys feel the need to hurt me? I just kept pretending to be OK. Yes, I was still hanging out, but I made sure I got home to get ready for school the next day. The guy that my mother was with, who later became her husband, continued to encourage me to make better life decisions so I stopped hanging out. Graduating high school became my goal.

*"*Arise, shine; for thy light is come, and the glory of the Lord is risen upon thee." Isaiah 60:1*

Throughout the remainder of my high school year, I met a guy through a family friend. This guy and I lived in different neighborhoods, and we also attended different high schools. We spent a lot of time together enjoying each other's company. After about a year of spending time together, this guy began expressing his feelings toward me. He would always tell me that he loved me and wanted to marry me. For a while, I didn't believe him because I was still unsure of myself. I didn't think it was possible for anyone to love me. I was just being careful not to let anyone else hurt me. How could he love me if I didn't love myself? That's the question that I couldn't answer at that time.

"There is no fear in love; but perfect love casteth out fear: because fear hath torment. He that feareth is not made perfect in love." 1 John 4:18

Not only did this guy continue to tell me that he cared for me, but he was also doing things that showed me that he cared. Yes, I was beginning to feel good about myself. If this is what love was supposed to feel like, this is what I wanted. My first love. I always looked forward to spending time with him. We were going to be together after we finished high school. That was our promise. But I later learned that real love only comes from the creator of love, the Holy Spirit.

Chapter 6: For Better or For Worse

"Behold, I set before you this day a blessing and a curse"
Deuteronomy 11:26

I was starting to live again. This guy made me feel like I was worth something. The first time he asked me for my "self", I told him no. At that point, I was afraid that he was going to take advantage of me just like the other guys did, but he didn't. He told me that he was going to wait until I was ready. No, he didn't rush me, and we were still spending time together. He continued to tell me that he loved me and that is when I *"thought"* I came back to life. I found out he was seeing someone else the entire time we were together. Betrayed, but in love. I just couldn't understand it. He said he was going to leave her because he wanted to be with me.

"My beloved spake, and said unto me, "Rise up, my love, my fair one, and come away." Song of Solomon 2:10

He kept his promise to leave her. And right after he left her, we were engaged to be married. He joined the military, and I was going to be with him. When I learned that I was pregnant, I was extremely happy. Not only was I going to be a wife, but I was also going be a mother. Unfortunately, that didn't happen. The arguments started. When I told him I was pregnant, that's when the arguments stopped but before he came home to share the moment, I miscarried because of a physical altercation. And to make matters worse, I found out that he started seeing to the other female again.

Betrayed again but I was still emotionally bonded. After I graduated from high school, I decided to relocate. I moved to California. I wanted to start a new life because all I had in Cleveland was nightmares.

"Wherefore let him that thinketh he standeth take heed lest he fall." 1 Corinthians 10:12

The young man and I kept in touch. While he was still in the military, I let him know that I no longer lived in Cleveland. He came out to visit me in California when he got his military pass. We discussed our situation and at that time I let him know that I no longer wanted to be with him, nor did I want to get married. We got into a verbal confrontation which became physical. After a few days went by, he had to return to his military base. We kept in touch, and I let him know that I moved back to Cleveland since I didn't accomplish anything in California. When I returned to Cleveland, I made plans to work and try to forget about my painful situation. Yes, I tried but it just didn't happen.

"For with God, nothing shall be impossible." Luke 1:37

While he was on another military leave, he contacted me and asked if we could go somewhere and talk, so of course, I agreed. He came to my house and took me back to his mom's house. After a few minutes of talking, he tried to kiss me and as I was pushing him away, he grabbed my face and pulled my lip with his teeth. The worst thing ever, his teeth went through my lip. When I put my hand over my face that's when he started punching me. Worthless, numb and lifeless again. He took me home the next morning with a swollen face and bruises on my body. During that time in my life, I couldn't see what I was doing wrong but when I began my walk with Christ and understood the value in His word, my weaknesses were revealed, and He showed me how to protect myself from the schemes of the enemy.

"Put on the whole armor of God, that ye may be able to stand against the wiles of the devil." Ephesians 6:11

I was tired of living. My life was full of shame, depression, and embarrassment. Could it get any worse? Yes, but I wasn't going to let it. At that point, I did what I "thought" was the right thing to do to protect myself, hurt others before they hurt me. In my heart I knew it was wrong but in my mind I didn't care. No one else seemed to care so why should I?

"LORD, make me to know mine end, and the measure of my days, what it is; That I may know how frail I am." Psalm 39:4

I started hanging out in neighborhood bars again, drinking and trying to do what everyone else was doing but I made sure I stayed away from the men. I had nothing but hate in my heart for all of them. I didn't show it, but I would not let anyone of them get close to me. If a guy said he liked me or gave me a compliment, I left him alone because I didn't care to hear the lies. Yes, men would tell lies just to get what they wanted, which was my "self". But no, not mine. If I wanted to give a guy my "self", it was by choice and not because he lied to try to get it. And no, I wasn't sharing my "self" with just any guy, if it was something I chose to do, I just did it. My low self-esteem, which was partially destroyed by the enemy, caused me to think and behave in that manner.

Wait, before I continue, let me remind you once again that this is my past. Those are just a few of the things that God has brought me through and I'm very thankful for his words of empowerment that has allowed me to share those situations that no longer belong to me so please do not judge my past.

"See now that I, even I, am he, and there is no god with me: I kill, and I make alive; I wound, and I heal: Neither is there any that can deliver out of my hand." Deuteronomy 32:39

Though I was dealing with low self-esteem, I continued to hang out but after a while I got tired of being around people. I hated everybody, even myself. It became so difficult for me to fake my pain, and drinking was making it worse. For a long time, I held on to my low self-esteem and the fake belief that I wasn't pretty or smart enough for any man to want me for anything other than my "self".

And though I was dealing with low self-esteem, I continued to hang out, but I was always careful of my surroundings. The enemy tried to make me believe that I wasn't worthy enough for any man to love me. This was not true for one person. My ex-husband. This man always told me that I was his favorite girl, but my low self-esteem and insecurities wouldn't let me believe him. And though I enjoyed spending time with him, the 15-year difference in our age wouldn't let me trust him and my mind wouldn't let me think that he was different from the men that hurt me. But his love was genuine. We enjoyed each other's family before he became my husband. He made sure I had everything I needed. He made me feel protected because he didn't want anything to happen to me. He loved me but I didn't know how to accept, process or return the love he had for me. I started behaving in ways that had nothing to do with love. I refused to let this man hurt me. It was just a matter of time before he hurt me or betrayed me just like those other men did. But that thought was a lie that I told myself. That man loved me, and because of my brokenness, it was too late for me to realize it.

"He that trusteth in his own heart is a fool: But whoso walketh wisely, he shall be delivered." Proverbs 28:26

This man loved me and the fact that I never addressed my personal hurts with him before we were married, he had no idea how internally broken I was. I destroyed a good thing. We were separated and then we were divorced. How painful was that? Very painful. It was at that time that I knew I needed to start doing something different. I thought if I stayed busy the pain would go away. Not by the earth's length. Being busy did not take away the pain. My heart, my mind and my spirit were broken, and I didn't think it was possible for me to be healed.

"Now then it is no more I that do it, but sin that dwelleth in me."
Romans 7:17

I tried to stay busy by working, hanging out and drinking again, but no matter how much I tried to hide behind my pain, it just wouldn't go away. I was hurting and I also hurt the only man who proved his love for me.

"Heal me, O LORD, and I shall be healed; save me, and I shall be saved: for thou art my praise." Jeremiah 17:14

When we try to suppress our pain by using other measures outside of God's word, we will experience a deeper level of pain. God's word is the only way to heal our inner pain. God knew my pain and he knows your pain. He healed me because he needed to use my pain for his purpose. I can't thank him enough for keeping his promise to never leave me comfortless.

"Thou shalt increase my greatness, and comfort me on every side." Psalm 71:21

Chapter 7: Let the Truth Begin

"Let integrity and uprightness preserve me; for I wait on thee." Psalm 25:21

I was so internally broken that I didn't realize how much pain I was experiencing. The enemy tried to make me believe that I was a bad person and that's why those situations happened to me. Being abandoned by my father, being molested, raped and sexually assaulted. Being physically abused for refusing to stay in a relationship with someone who lied and cheated. The enemy is such a liar. I will admit that it was my fault for hurting the only man who showed me that I was worth loving.

"Unto *thee, O Lord, do I lift my soul." Psalm 25:1

I continued to see the man I cheated on my ex-husband with and of course that didn't turn out as expected. There were a lot of unhealthy things going on in that situation and although we discussed the issues, we still decided to end the situation. Unfortunately, that was another confrontation that left me with bruises. That was the end of my feelings. At that point, I began to believe that my life was useless. If there was a God, why did he let me experience so much trauma, pain and confusion?

"For whosoever shall call upon the name of the Lord shall be saved." Romans 10:13

I tried to attend church again, but I kept thinking God wouldn't care enough to know about me or understand what I was going through. Who was I? If he cared, those things wouldn't have happened to me. I was so uncomfortable being around the people in church because I thought God only cared for them and even though I still didn't understand the meaning of all that *"stuff"*, God understood me.

Sadly, I stopped going to church and I found myself hanging out in bars again, trying to "fit in" but something within me wouldn't let me totally give in to the mess of hanging out and drinking. The nightmares would surface after a few drinks, and those nightmares let me know that the bars were not the place for me. I didn't want to live the rest of my life dealing with those nightmares and pretending to be OK. I felt like I was living in the wilderness. Yes, I was walking in the dark shadow of my heart.

"Watch ye and pray, lest ye enter into temptation, the spirit truly is ready, but the flesh is weak." Mark 14:36

Walking in the shadow of my heart caused me to slip into the arms of someone who was "bound by marriage." Yes, someone whom I thought could help ease my pain. We shared good times through laughter and fun outings, but the pain, emptiness and loneliness were still lingering because this "someone" had other obligations.

"But the Lord is faithful, who shall stablish you, and keep you from evil." 2 Thessalonians 3:3

As I was trying to find my way out of the wilderness with my broken heart, I cried out to God. He heard my voice, and he rescued me. He gave me what I needed to find my way through the darkness, but he said forgiveness was the only way to escape the dangers of wandering in the wilderness. I was already blinded by pain, misery and emotional stress, what else could go wrong. I decided to take heed to his instruction and follow the light.

"And God shall wipe away all tears from their eyes; and there shall be no more death, neither sorrow, nor crying, neither shall there be any more pain: for the former things are passed away." Revelations 21:4

Even though I didn't quite understand God's instructions, I knew I had to trust and obey him if I wanted to escape any unseen dangers. God continued to shine the light of his grace and mercies on the path that led me to safety. His spirit of truth enhanced my vision to build a foundation of faith through the power of his unconditional love. A love that was difficult for me to believe existed. But how could God love me and allow me to hurt? Well, God said to me, "I needed your pain to prove my loyalty."

"To open their eyes, and to turn them from darkness to light, and from the power of Satan unto God, that they may receive forgiveness of sins, and inheritance among them which are sanctified by faith that is in me." Acts 26:18

The first light that I thought would take away my vision was asking for forgiveness from the wife of the one who was bound by marriage, but the enemy was still trying to set traps to lure me into being disobedient. Forgiveness was accepted and it was so. God began to clear the path that led me safely out of the dark shadow of my heart.

We know how uncomfortable is to forgive or ask for forgiveness, so it is extremely important to adhere to God's instructions. If you trust God for who he is, he will guide you through the process because he knows that you cannot do it in your own strength.

"In whom we hath redemption through his blood, even the forgiveness of sins." Colossians 1:14

Forgiving doesn't make the situations okay nor does it make you look foolish. God's word teaches us that forgiving makes it possible for us to be used in ways that's beyond our imagination. An unforgiving heart and a broken spirit are stumbling blocks that interferes with the work that God needs to do through his children.

Chapter 8: Forgiving to Forgive

"But if ye do not forgive, neither will your Father which is in heaven forgive your trespasses." Mark 11:26

Though I stopped going to church at that time, I always remembered some things I was taught about forgiveness. I started studying the bible and reading a lot of self-help books to try to change my life so that I could feel better about myself. For some natural reason, I started hearing more stories about people who experienced situations that were like mine and some that were worse than mine and how their life changed after forgiving the person that hurt them. Well, I thought to myself, that's them, not me. I didn't do anything wrong, and I wasn't going to look like a fool trying to forgive anybody who hurt me. Those men were crazy, not me and forgiving them was never going to happen. Not by the earth's length. I guess I'll have to keep pretending to be OK. Well, that was another confusing trap that the enemy tried to set.

"Show me thy ways, O Lord, teach me thy path." Psalm 25:4

Those men may have been unaware of the negative impact that their foul behavior had on my mental and emotional development. I prayed and asked God to forgive those men. I also had to forgive each one of them in my heart because that's where I experienced most of my pain. From the emotional neglect by my father's absence to the physical abuse I experienced in those unfortunate situations. It wasn't easy but I had to forgive them, and I thought that was all I had to do. Nope, it was more to the process than I imagined. Not only did I forgive them, but God also needed me to pray for them. Wait, who does that and why? Now forgiving was one thing but I had to pray for them. The only way for me to get complete healing was to pray for them. No, no, no and nope. Not by the earth's length. I guess I'll have to live the rest of my life in pain. Shame on the enemy because that was another trap he tried to set.

I forgave those men, and I also prayed for their healing. The enemy that was on a prowl to try to destroy my spirit, was the same enemy that was on a mission to attack the minds of those men. God revealed to me that everyone is susceptible to the enemy's attack, and unfortunately, those men were on the enemy's radar for mental manipulation.

The most interesting part of this forgiving and praying process is that it didn't have to be done face to face. The process took place in my heart because that's where the pain needed to be removed.

"If ye abide in me, and my words abide in you, ye shall ask what ye will, and it shall be done unto you." John 15:7

Forgiving didn't mean that I was supposed to forget, it was meant for the purpose of supporting me on my spiritual journey. God carried me through those situations while preparing me for the purpose he had for my life. God also had a purpose for the life of each one of those men because he created each one of us for a purpose. I also asked God to forgive me for the pain I caused my ex-husband. After I shared my past experiences with him, I asked him if he would forgive me and he said yes, and it was so. God's grace through forgiveness gave me the freedom to live.

"In the day when I cried, thou answeredst me, and strengthenedst me with strength in my soul." Psalm 138:3

Although no one in my family was aware of the situations I experienced, it was difficult for me to understand those things myself. Being numb to my own feelings, I really thought that was the way I was supposed to feel. Yes, another confusing trap the enemy tried to set.

"He brought me forth also into a large place; He delivered me, because he delighted in me." Psalm 18:19

Yes, my mom talked to me (as a child) about the spirit of God and Jesus being the Son of God. No, I didn't understand those teachings about God when I was a child, but I am so glad and honored to know about him now. Those feelings that was making me "pretend to be OK" was the spirit of God giving me the strength to keep winning the battle against the enemy that hates the truth about every good thing God created.

The enemy's intention is to hurt us so he will look for ways to slip into our thoughts and that's why God instructs us to be mindful of the enemy's tactics to use our weakness to try to set dangerous traps of confusion and manipulation. When we are walking by faith, we are careful not to fall prey to enemy's traps.

God let me know that the perfect cure for the pain I experienced from all those situations was his perfect timing. His Holy Spirit showed up at the right time during each experience. What a blessing it is to know that God will keep his promise to "never forsake us."

"And he that sat upon the throne said, Behold, I make all things new. And he said unto me, Write: for these words are true and faithful." Revelations 21:5

How amazing it is to be healed, blessed and highly favored by God.

"And God shall wipe away all tears from their eyes; and there shall be no more death, neither sorrow, nor crying, neither shall there be any more pain: for the former things are passed away." Revelations 21:4

God is a jealous God, and he needs you to remain confident in Him by quieting your mind, seeking him in silence and being willing to be proactive in transforming your thoughts by standing firm on his word and increasing your faith to renew your spirit.

Not By Myself

"Now unto him that is able to keep you from falling, and to present you faultless before the presence of his glory with exceeding joy." Jude 1:24

God had a distinctive way of letting me know how good he is, and the enemy almost made me think that I was not on God's radar. The trauma I experienced made me afraid to walk in God's will for my life but when I realized that *"He is before all things, and by him all things consist," Colossians 1:17,* and He found me worthy of everything he created me to be, I began to walk in the value he placed on my life.

"Bless the Lord O my soul: and all that is within me, bless his holy name." Psalm 103:1

All those stressful situations caused me a lot of pain and to hurt others, but forgiveness has prevailed because the mighty hand of God has broken the chains of the enemy's stronghold and freed me to glorify his goodness. His word is the best gift that he freely gives us. His word is everything.

"In the beginning was the Word and the Word was with God, and the Word was God." John 1:1

Not By Yourself

"And I will put my spirit within you, and cause you to walk in my statutes, and ye shall keep my judgments, and do them."
Ezekiel 36:27

Sometimes you may think, feel, or believe that life is a big challenge, and I am so happy to inform you that it is. If you have faced or are facing a traumatic situation, you may be tempted to think that you are defenseless to the enemy's traps. The very thing you want for yourself is to feel safe and protected but when the enemy sets traps for emotional manipulation, neglect, bullying, or physical abuse, you may also be tempted to believe that your life is worthless. Adults as well as children who have fallen prey to these traps tend to believe that they are powerless to their personal feelings because of the fear of being misunderstood. But God is ready to renew your mind, heart and spirit.

"37Nay, in all these things we are more than conquerors through him that loved us. 38For I am persuaded, that neither death, nor life, nor angels, nor principalities, nor powers, nor things present, nor things to come, 39nor height, nor depth, nor any other creature, shall be able to separate us from the love of God, which is in Christ Jesus our Lord." Romans 8:37-39

God knows your heart because he knows himself so allow him to be the strength you deserve. God is love, he's an encourager, and a healer. God also promised to be everything you need to help you move your mountains.

When you make the choice to let God use your circumstances to uplift his Kingdom, you'll make room in your life to prove God's perfect will. If you honestly love God in the way that you say, then you must allow him to accept you just the way you are. He created you in the image of his likeness, so he already knows everything about you.

"Who hath put wisdom in the inward parts? Or hath given understanding to the heart?" Job 38:36

If you are ready to move your mountains and overcome your past disappointments, make yourself available to God. Be willing to put your trust in his word. It's time for you to shame the enemy by acknowledging the new life that God has uniquely established just for you. You now have the power, wisdom, and the confidence to walk in the fruits of the spirit which are:

"22Love, joy, peace, longsuffering, gentleness, goodness, faith, 23meekness, temperance: against such there is no law. 24And they that are Christ's have crucified the flesh with the affections and lusts. 25If we live in the Spirit, let us also walk in the Spirit." Galatians 5:22-25

Not By Yourself

"And I will strengthen them in the Lord; and they shall walk up and down in his name, saith the Lord." Zechariah 10:12

When you choose to honor God through your situations, he will equip you with the power to shame the enemy. This section was designed to encourage you to open your heart and move forward by faith. This is your healing journey, and you are not obligated to share this information with anyone. Being honest with your heart is your only requirement so:

Let your journey begin:

"For we through the Spirit wait for the hope of righteousness by faith." Galatians 5:5

What is the *worst* thing that *will* happen when you *trust* God?

_____

What part of you are you still withholding from God?

_____

How much value does your past add to your present moment?

_____

How have you planned to establish a personal support system?

_____

How often do you evaluate your emotional health?

If you could change 1 thing about yourself, what would it be? Why?

Do you see beauty in God's creation? Why? Why not?

How does your intuition promote your healing?

What benefits are you receiving through unforgiveness?

How have you planned to celebrate your new life?

"¹⁰When wisdom entereth into thine heart, and knowledge is pleasant unto thy soul; ¹¹Discretion shall preserve thee, understanding shall keep thee." Proverbs 2:10-11

God has searched for your heart, and he found it. God loves you and he will follow through with his plans. Your life has so much value. If you find yourself experiencing doubt or fear, don't give up. The enemy is attracted to emotional stress so be aware of your thoughts and your personal environment because he will find a way to use something or someone that is dear to your heart to attack your spirit. Humble your spirit so you can distract the enemy. Receive God's promise through his grace, mercy and his everlasting love.

"And it shall come to pass that whosoever shall call on the name of the Lord shall be saved." Acts 2:21

Take advantage of everything that will help you build and maintain a healthy spiritual life. When you embrace the new life that you were created for, your strength and confidence will also have a positive impact on the lives of others.

Honoring Your Gift

"And God said, Let there be light; and there was light."
Genesis 1:3

At some point in our lives, we have all been given a unique or special gift. Whether it was a birthday gift, Christmas gift or just a gift of appreciation, someone took their time and effort to select the perfect gift that they felt would add value to our life. If we liked the gift and it came with instructions, we made the time to read the instructions to learn how to use it. *Galatians 5:22-23* says that the fruits of the spirit, which are spiritual gifts from God, adds value to your life. These spiritual gifts will protect you from the dangers of falling prey to the enemy's attempt to distract you from acknowledging and receiving instructions on how to use your gift to uplift God's Kingdom.

Honor your gift by making yourself available for God to use you. Let God cleanse your heart daily so you can stay connected to source of your new life. When you establish a strong spiritual foundation, you can begin to master effective levels of God's wisdom that will help you live a peaceful life according to His will.

"For the wages of sin is death, but the gift of God is eternal life through Jesus Christ our Lord." Romans 6:23

Honoring Your Gift

"A man's gift maketh room for him, And bringeth him before great men." Proverbs 18:16

I believe in you, and I believe in your gift. When you acknowledge the gift that God has specifically designed for you, he will supply you with everything you need that will help you master your gift. The section below was also created to motivate and encourage you to establish a personal foundation that may help you to recognize and honor the gift that God has blessed you with. When you decide to actively live the life that God intended for you, your past hurts, traumas, and disappointments will become obsolete. Let's make time to:

Let Your Gift Uplift the Kingdom:

What values have you placed on your gift?

_____

How does your gift influence your daily activities?

_____

What strategies have you planned to use to enrich your gift?

_____

What is your plan to set boundaries around your personal time?

_____

How have you planned to use your gift to benefit others?

_____

Purpose or Potential, which one holds more value for you?

_____

What outcome are you going to achieve by honoring your gift?

_____

What is your fear of success?

_____

How have you planned to align your needs with your gift?

_____

How have you planned to integrate your faith with your gift?

_____

Your gift is priceless. If there was no truth in it, I would not have had the courage to use my gift to share my testimony and I also believe that God wants to use your testimony for his glory.

"But I have prayed for thee, that thy faith fail not: and when thou art converted, strengthen thy brethren." Luke 22:32

"And God said, Let there be light: and there was light" Genesis 1:3

y	q	a	f	s	a	n	c	t	i	f	i	e	d	n	b	x	t	z	l
o	b	k	e	s	r	q	o	v	p	x	h	i	l	t	s	v	y	i	u
n	k	l	y	d	x	i	l	q	e	g	v	c	h	s	f	r	g	z	k
t	n	v	e	p	s	q	v	i	a	c	f	t	i	n	z	h	u	f	o
d	l	c	z	s	g	e	q	j	c	y	b	r	o	v	t	f	p	h	n
e	b	x	o	g	s	j	u	n	e	b	p	o	s	a	u	t	n	v	i
v	c	y	a	o	l	e	y	q	i	f	d	b	y	x	j	x	s	t	a
r	l	t	f	d	y	g	d	v	x	a	e	p	b	e	i	u	z	n	o
e	f	l	j	k	q	b	s	z	g	w	u	i	n	r	u	o	v	a	f
s	n	r	q	a	t	z	h	p	j	i	o	q	f	s	d	l	k	n	t
e	r	z	m	e	r	c	i	f	u	l	j	b	o	i	z	u	a	e	c
r	g	f	d	k	o	i	q	e	o	s	i	b	n	x	l	g	t	v	y
p	y	i	s	a	q	z	i	y	k	e	t	o	x	i	n	k	e	o	f
a	h	j	v	r	o	x	p	y	z	i	f	g	d	q	a	l	t	c	d
s	z	j	e	f	n	e	v	a	e	h	d	o	l	c	y	r	a	x	o

1) Blessed	6) Merciful
2) Covenant	7) Peace
3) Favour	8) Preserved
4) Heaven	9) Rainbow
5) Light	10) Sanctified

j	r	t	n	h	o	l	y	k	b	v	z	q	y	j	p	s	d	a	i
x	i	k	v	n	f	x	o	u	s	a	q	c	s	f	t	y	b	e	s
c	g	f	j	o	q	d	j	i	v	a	z	t	y	l	k	b	r	c	o
f	h	o	s	q	y	g	k	f	l	b	n	h	f	z	e	x	t	s	q
a	t	v	y	x	n	v	t	i	q	e	k	p	o	a	r	z	h	l	t
i	e	o	q	u	p	s	n	f	m	t	n	s	d	y	q	i	v	p	x
t	o	u	n	r	c	s	e	d	h	k	p	a	s	s	o	v	e	r	s
h	u	y	q	z	h	v	n	e	o	b	u	i	v	c	d	q	k	f	a
f	s	z	p	i	u	a	d	c	s	j	e	y	k	d	i	l	q	z	c
u	n	t	a	s	m	h	o	i	p	r	n	q	i	j	f	b	e	n	r
l	e	v	h	m	b	i	x	o	t	n	b	e	h	l	s	u	g	l	i
z	s	f	o	r	l	t	o	j	y	i	x	n	e	v	i	g	r	o	f
o	s	c	v	x	e	n	u	e	d	q	h	p	z	a	s	u	l	x	i
t	b	r	n	c	d	k	q	r	e	i	t	d	f	z	o	r	t	k	c
f	e	s	d	q	s	e	i	n	o	m	i	t	s	e	t	a	z	i	e

1) Commandments   6) Passover

2) Faithful   7) Rejoice

3) Forgiven   8) Righteousness

4) Holy   9) Sacrifice

5) Humbled   10) Testimonies

"There is none Holy as the LORD:" 1 Samuel 2:2

p	g	a	l	v	t	d	i	q	e	p	o	h	k	f	t	k	a	p	o
f	e	i	h	a	j	s	n	e	k	z	q	u	i	h	v	t	d	g	r
i	a	r	q	x	u	t	j	k	n	y	a	i	v	t	e	b	v	k	u
y	c	d	s	r	f	s	l	g	r	k	o	z	n	c	q	f	e	z	t
z	p	v	f	i	d	u	x	h	a	n	n	a	h	r	i	k	r	q	d
o	i	z	g	v	s	r	b	a	z	i	f	v	n	q	l	y	s	c	f
v	y	d	u	b	k	t	i	r	s	k	q	u	s	o	k	g	i	l	y
u	h	e	b	i	q	o	e	v	a	x	c	l	i	d	f	t	t	d	r
a	p	d	o	k	v	s	b	n	f	t	g	n	y	h	s	e	y	l	x
i	v	i	p	a	q	c	x	y	c	n	a	e	x	t	u	v	e	o	a
r	x	c	g	o	i	f	d	s	l	e	i	r	v	n	s	f	y	i	k
d	v	a	e	q	z	h	q	x	c	r	d	a	j	i	t	e	z	r	u
o	k	t	y	s	f	b	k	i	z	r	j	b	o	n	c	v	n	q	e
h	r	e	d	n	e	r	r	u	s	a	n	l	f	a	u	v	p	o	k
u	y	d	f	r	x	i	q	u	l	b	i	e	h	n	g	z	s	a	h

1) Adversity
2) Barren
3) Dedicated
4) Hannah
5) Honest

6) Hope
7) Persistence
8) Surrender
9) Trust
10) Vulnerable

v	n	x	s	c	e	q	f	p	z	a	o	y	s	d	y	k	u	l	h
o	j	e	h	o	v	a	h	j	i	r	e	h	r	t	q	f	d	p	e
i	b	e	q	m	z	y	h	o	c	v	e	s	r	i	l	t	r	x	a
r	d	s	g	p	l	f	e	x	y	e	s	h	u	a	i	f	s	x	l
e	h	f	i	a	r	j	o	s	r	z	n	e	a	r	k	q	v	n	e
m	s	c	z	s	e	b	y	t	a	v	f	r	d	q	i	h	l	t	r
e	x	s	r	s	y	f	h	i	q	v	z	n	o	j	t	i	o	q	a
e	f	l	o	i	k	s	a	v	o	x	e	j	g	d	b	l	s	a	z
d	g	i	t	o	b	a	j	b	z	i	q	s	f	t	r	e	b	c	i
e	x	p	f	n	c	f	e	s	r	c	a	z	o	q	v	u	i	f	e
r	d	s	r	a	q	d	i	f	h	b	f	v	n	r	s	n	t	d	z
q	x	b	a	t	i	e	r	t	s	h	k	f	o	s	c	a	y	z	f
o	y	v	n	e	f	s	u	s	e	j	o	k	s	l	d	m	g	t	s
t	p	g	n	v	a	t	i	d	f	s	l	i	n	r	i	m	h	x	u
a	k	t	r	i	q	y	b	j	i	t	f	s	h	l	q	i	t	r	x

1) Compassionate
2) Friend
3) Healer
4) Immanuel
5) Jehovah-Jireh

6) Jesus
7) Obedient
8) Redeemer
9) Son Of God
10) Yeshua

"And if I perish, I perish;" Esther 4:16

e	c	x	a	n	s	q	c	t	h	k	f	a	s	t	i	n	g	u	i
s	n	g	f	y	r	k	f	b	e	l	q	i	x	p	j	o	r	s	e
v	y	i	g	h	a	s	s	a	d	a	h	v	n	r	d	f	s	u	l
m	f	t	p	i	c	r	z	n	h	e	v	g	f	s	q	a	c	y	o
b	o	h	s	z	v	x	y	q	o	r	y	h	x	t	n	s	p	l	r
i	b	r	q	j	h	r	p	u	q	x	f	s	y	a	p	x	i	b	p
f	s	i	d	x	a	q	y	e	a	l	i	a	h	i	b	a	p	o	h
v	q	n	g	e	y	s	d	t	x	t	u	y	e	q	f	c	r	j	a
t	g	e	a	f	c	v	p	o	v	s	a	q	b	x	t	e	y	l	n
u	c	e	r	b	r	a	v	e	h	z	n	t	k	f	n	o	c	z	y
k	y	u	t	s	p	y	i	a	f	j	e	q	t	r	l	w	i	h	r
d	f	q	s	n	j	e	q	b	n	y	k	i	l	d	h	s	o	a	j
b	v	x	e	t	q	u	x	a	o	u	f	y	q	v	t	g	k	r	e
i	j	f	s	x	k	y	r	e	q	i	z	o	n	k	p	i	f	t	c
r	x	a	q	n	o	i	t	i	t	e	p	n	t	f	r	e	i	u	h

1) Abihail
2) Banquet
3) Brave
4) Crown
5) Fasting

6) Hadassah
7) Mordecai
8) Orphan
9) Petition
10) Queen

"I know that thou canst do everything," Job 42:2

a	r	d	s	h	j	i	q	g	s	f	s	v	i	l	r	d	j	n	k
j	f	b	o	c	x	e	l	v	b	p	e	f	o	q	z	a	o	u	g
r	k	f	s	g	f	e	i	z	a	v	r	n	j	y	f	t	b	k	s
o	b	x	l	e	d	s	k	t	y	o	v	q	i	n	s	a	f	r	z
h	u	j	s	i	x	e	n	u	i	y	a	o	p	e	r	f	e	c	t
i	p	x	v	q	c	f	b	j	c	l	n	g	d	t	x	p	q	o	s
l	r	v	s	y	a	t	r	s	l	q	t	h	i	c	l	f	o	z	a
c	i	t	n	t	q	k	i	x	e	o	a	f	y	n	i	b	d	s	f
u	g	v	f	i	e	q	y	o	a	t	p	z	s	j	r	k	l	f	d
x	h	s	y	r	p	a	k	i	n	s	a	v	r	e	d	s	o	t	e
k	t	c	x	g	e	u	y	r	j	f	t	i	x	e	z	t	q	v	t
g	b	f	a	e	q	n	i	e	b	d	j	p	s	k	f	r	u	a	s
u	o	v	s	t	p	r	f	q	g	z	x	r	a	q	n	g	t	f	j
c	b	z	x	n	a	k	i	s	o	r	u	j	n	x	o	r	e	y	q
h	f	a	v	i	d	y	q	b	z	c	a	h	p	u	w	i	s	e	

1) Affliction   6) Perfect

2) Clean   7) Servant

3) Cursed   8) Stedfast

4) Integrity   9) Upright

5) Job   10) Wise

"I cried by reason of mine affliction unto the LORD," Jonah 2:2

y	i	c	s	o	a	x	b	u	k	s	t	o	r	m	h	z	a	j	k
t	r	d	g	b	j	f	n	z	s	q	g	d	a	k	i	r	d	o	f
n	v	a	j	q	x	y	u	w	h	a	l	e	i	p	b	t	f	p	e
g	o	u	r	d	c	t	h	n	s	p	q	c	h	k	l	u	o	p	z
i	b	y	s	o	v	g	a	o	f	t	y	r	e	k	i	q	z	a	s
e	z	d	g	r	e	d	v	a	o	r	s	k	i	j	n	t	s	f	o
r	b	o	c	s	c	x	a	k	d	h	e	v	e	n	i	n	q	k	e
e	j	f	s	r	n	q	b	l	a	e	q	s	f	g	o	y	i	n	h
v	g	u	c	x	a	h	t	n	q	l	t	k	t	y	b	z	t	o	s
o	y	e	s	f	t	z	o	l	g	s	e	n	i	o	j	x	e	r	i
s	f	c	a	k	n	j	o	f	x	p	t	z	f	y	o	k	q	a	h
g	n	s	u	h	e	q	b	t	v	u	i	p	s	o	f	d	c	z	s
o	v	t	g	s	p	h	e	j	a	f	j	g	v	d	k	e	t	q	r
j	s	o	q	n	e	i	s	f	p	r	o	p	h	e	t	a	j	z	a
h	t	r	e	y	r	u	l	w	h	b	f	o	a	n	i	y	u	x	t

1) Gourd
2) Jonah
3) Joppa
4) Nineveh
5) Prophet

6) Repentance
7) Sovereignty
8) Storm
9) Tarshish
10) Whale

"And the LORD was with Joseph;" Genesis 39:2

b	f	g	u	v	s	i	l	p	x	r	o	l	a	f	q	z	o	i	j
r	x	b	s	z	f	q	t	o	x	g	k	i	c	e	e	x	z	s	o
l	r	e	w	o	p	k	z	t	u	q	b	x	h	s	d	e	u	y	s
u	d	t	o	z	r	f	v	i	j	e	z	k	q	y	r	l	f	h	e
f	c	r	g	x	t	e	q	p	y	c	h	l	t	d	x	f	g	y	p
s	x	a	c	t	d	a	k	h	f	y	v	n	i	q	o	c	k	h	h
s	v	y	h	g	t	f	n	a	l	z	e	i	b	t	f	r	q	t	c
e	o	e	x	r	q	y	b	r	f	m	v	g	x	a	b	j	i	r	u
c	y	d	u	b	k	h	p	i	g	z	a	h	r	q	o	f	p	o	y
c	f	b	z	a	s	h	t	r	n	q	k	i	b	e	s	v	a	w	o
u	t	c	q	g	p	b	e	o	i	r	f	s	k	v	m	a	u	t	n
s	x	r	l	x	a	c	t	f	d	h	k	s	p	c	z	a	t	s	e
g	b	a	p	v	s	e	f	h	n	x	q	z	h	f	c	l	e	u	t
i	t	n	e	i	t	a	p	e	z	v	a	l	j	s	q	o	j	r	k
x	p	r	d	o	f	e	u	i	r	e	s	i	l	i	e	n	t	t	d

1) Betrayed

2) Discernment

3) Dreamer

4) Joseph

5) Patient

6) Potiphar

7) Power

8) Resilient

9) Successful

10) Trustworthy

f	x	v	b	g	y	p	o	z	b	x	v	i	c	t	o	r	y	q	p
j	r	h	t	a	v	o	e	x	i	h	g	q	m	k	t	a	c	f	a
i	p	z	x	q	r	l	e	v	i	z	e	i	n	p	f	h	r	g	l
b	n	h	g	z	y	a	x	s	b	a	l	n	f	e	o	x	d	s	m
i	v	f	k	t	p	z	k	a	h	i	g	s	y	c	n	u	k	l	t
y	x	e	g	f	q	o	d	e	t	c	i	p	t	h	l	x	v	y	r
d	f	q	c	b	o	f	r	a	c	x	k	i	q	s	t	h	z	j	e
e	j	q	i	a	v	i	r	x	f	e	a	r	l	e	s	s	k	u	e
b	k	v	g	t	p	y	d	r	e	q	x	a	n	u	i	g	b	j	l
o	r	b	e	a	l	r	q	a	x	v	r	t	e	b	f	v	r	u	s
r	c	y	t	e	r	a	n	c	p	f	e	i	s	k	b	z	a	d	i
a	v	y	a	q	k	s	x	f	e	p	v	o	z	r	l	n	v	g	y
h	g	d	r	z	f	e	y	p	v	q	j	n	b	a	t	j	z	e	o
q	e	v	t	b	a	x	t	n	j	g	e	r	n	d	o	x	e	l	k
r	j	f	s	z	o	c	h	t	g	s	s	e	t	e	h	p	o	r	p

1) Barak
2) Deborah
3) Fearless
4) Inspiration
5) Judge

6) Military Leader
7) Palm Tree
8) Prophetess
9) Strategic
10) Victory

"But Noah found grace in the eyes of the LORD." Genesis 6:8

y	r	a	x	q	c	b	c	h	j	o	t	l	v	r	e	x	o	g	d
a	e	c	d	r	x	h	l	q	s	n	a	e	x	o	p	q	c	h	o
a	r	g	o	j	d	a	q	e	o	y	y	b	n	l	r	b	v	n	v
z	x	k	c	y	p	t	o	i	b	u	i	q	x	z	o	s	j	p	e
i	k	f	z	a	b	v	t	c	p	k	o	i	b	i	v	u	h	b	l
k	b	j	s	e	r	a	k	g	s	l	i	u	t	r	i	v	s	z	j
p	n	v	c	s	v	l	r	q	n	o	a	h	n	v	s	b	g	i	r
d	h	b	u	l	f	k	j	b	v	l	z	k	d	r	i	x	y	t	p
a	q	j	a	n	z	y	x	k	j	i	u	q	o	d	o	j	i	n	d
z	y	s	u	j	v	z	i	r	e	v	o	s	o	t	n	u	b	e	a
g	i	p	q	e	b	n	z	y	i	e	l	d	l	p	h	a	f	m	t
f	h	s	c	z	g	i	j	q	a	l	o	t	f	x	t	y	n	g	i
k	n	a	d	s	p	a	v	z	u	e	i	b	o	l	h	g	a	d	q
l	r	f	z	y	n	r	j	q	f	a	l	h	q	a	i	k	s	u	x
g	z	s	d	o	r	x	n	v	z	f	p	o	j	r	e	x	t	j	a

1) Ark   6) Noah

2) Dove   7) Olive Leaf

3) Flood   8) Provision

4) Grace   9) Rain

5) Judgment   10) Salvation

Personal Accomplishment

Personal Accomplishment

Personal Accomplishment

Personal Accomplishment

_____

_____

_____

_____

_____

_____

_____

_____

_____

_____

_____

_____

_____

_____

_____

_____

_____

_____

_____

_____

_____

Personal Accomplishment

Personal Accomplishment

_____

_____

_____

_____

_____

_____

_____

_____

_____

_____

_____

_____

_____

_____

_____

_____

_____

Personal Accomplishment

Personal Accomplishment

Personal Accomplishment

_____

_____

_____

_____

_____

_____

_____

_____

_____

_____

_____

_____

_____

_____

_____

_____

_____

_____

_____

_____

Personal Accomplishment

I believe in God for your renewed mind and heart, and I am so excited for you. He is the glory of your life, and I pray that you will enjoy the new life that he has blessed you with.

Again, all the information that's shared throughout this book is based upon my personal experiences and my healing journey. The names of my perpetrators have not been mentioned and it's only by the grace of God that everyone has been forgiven.

"When you find joy during the dark times, the sun will find pleasure rising in the depth of your heart. A bright spirit cannot hide in darkness because the light will illuminate from the secret corners of your mind."

Lanatha Johnson

As a reminder, all information shared throughout this book is not intended to be used as a resource to diagnose or cure any illness and neither am I licensed therapist or counselor.

Made in the USA
Columbia, SC
24 January 2026

77951340R00055